Rental Property Investing

Maximize Profit and Minimize Headache with Your First Rental Properties

Table of Contents

quality. Trademarks that are mentioned are done without written consent and can in no way be considered an endorsement from the trademark holder.

Introduction

Congratulations on acquiring *Rental Property Investing* and thank you for doing so.

The following chapters will discuss everything that you need to know to get started in rental property investing. This is a unique form of investing that allows you to hold a tangible property, earning equity in the property while still making a profit at the same time. It can also be really rewarding, allowing you a chance to work hard and see your money reflect this.

There are many aspects that you will need to consider before getting into rental property investing and this guidebook will take the time to look at each benefit. Inside we will discuss some of the basics of getting started in this kind of investing, the different options you have in types of rental properties, how to fix up the rental property, picking the perfect rental price to cover your costs and still make a profit, and how to pick the perfect tenants to avoid problems down the line.

While rental property investing is not the best option for everyone, it can be extremely rewarding and is a good way to grow your investing portfolio and replace your full time income. When you are ready to add rental properties to your portfolio, make sure to read through this guidebook to learn everything that you need to get started.

There are plenty of books on this subject on the market, thanks again for choosing this one! Every effort was made to ensure it is full of as much useful information as possible, please enjoy!

Chapter 1:
Getting Into Rental Property Investing

Rental properties are a good way to start investing your money while building up some equity at the same time. You will be in possession of the property the whole time, making it easy to do what you would like with the property, while still making money at the same time.

But there are a lot of things you have to keep track of when it comes to a rental property. As a landlord, you have certain responsibilities to your tenants and must maintain your properties as well. Ensuring that rent is enough to cover your costs, that the property doesn't sit vacant for long, and that you pick good tenants can add to the workload of this investment.

Before jumping into rental property investing, it is important to understand that there is some work along with the income. Too many beginners assume that they can jump into the market and make a lot of money with very little work. While rental property investing can be a great way to make some of that extra money, it does require a bit of work as well. Before getting into this investment, take a look at some of the benefits and negatives to fully understand your choices.

Benefits

Rental property investing is a type of business. You will have to serve a customer (the tenant) by providing them with a safe and well kept place to live and they will pay you for these services. From this perspective, there are four benefits that you can consider when choosing to go with this investment including:

- Tax advantages

- Appreciation

- Current income

- Tangible asset

Tangible Asset

Unlike some other investments, rental properties are tangible products, something that you are able to touch and see. With other investment options, such as owning shares in a company, you can step into the home you rent, go and make changes, and see it any time that you want. Rental properties give you a home and land to work with and if the rental part doesn't work out, you can always resell the house and recover your losses. Many people appreciate rental investing because they like owning a property they can actually see.

Current Income

Rental properties allow you to make an income right now, rather than later on when you sell a home. The amount of income will depend on how much you charge for rent minus what you pay for in mortgage and other expenses to keep the house running. In the beginning, your expenses will include at least the mortgage, though over time you may pay this off and can keep more money in your pocket. You also need to consider taxes, insurance, and any utilities you plan to pay out of packet.

Picking out where to place the rent for your property can be tough. You have to look at your current costs and figure out how much income you would like to make. Plus, it is important that rent stays within market value or you will never get someone in the door to use your property. Most of the time if you pick out the right property and keep your mortgage amount low (many landlords don't pay for utilities for their tenants), you can keep the rent at market levels and still make a profit.

Equity

One of the benefits of doing rental properties rather than flipping homes is that you can build equity over time. Basically, equity is the difference between what your property is worth and what you owe on the property. The more you pay off the mortgage, the more equity you have. And since most real estate increases in value over time, you can really build up equity fast.

Now, there are a few things that you can do with this equity. Some landlords will build up the equity and then take out that amount in cash to use on purchasing new property or for other needs. This is an easy cash flow system, as long as you pay it back, without having to jump through as many hoops with the bank.

You can build up equity by paying off the mortgage, or you can do so with making updates to the home. Purchasing a dilapidated old home and fixing it up to match the rest of the neighborhood can quickly increase the equity of a home faster than just paying off the mortgage. Adding more value to the home, such as a new roof, an addition to the home, or more land to go with it, can add more equity. And simply holding onto the home and taking care of it for a number of years can add more equity because the real estate market all goes up.

This equity can help you to grow your business or can return a bigger profit if you decide to sell the home down the line. And all of this occurs while you are making a profit from your current tenant.

Tax Advantages

There are numerous tax advantages that come with rental properties. This is a business so you will be able to deduct expenses that occur while keeping the house up and running. You can claim your mortgage, taxes, and interest rate when tax season comes. And working with a tax professional makes it easier to find the best deductions that will save you even more money, even while you are make a profit.

The trick here is to use your tax advantages the right way. Instead of going out and using that money to buy something crazy, reinvest it in your properties. Get some maintenance work done, set it aside in a savings account to go towards obtaining another property, or use it in another way to further your current investment.

Risks of using rental properties

While there benefits to using rental property investment, there are some risks that can make it hard to earn the money you want in real estate. The main risks that you may face include:

Bad tenants

- Unexpected expenses

- Liability

- Vacancy

- Attorney fees

- Advertising fees

- Eviction expenses

Liability

As a landlord, there are certain circumstances that can cost you more in insurance claims and unexpected expenses. If something happens to a tenant on the property due to an oversight on your part, you could pay more money out of pocket. You will be responsible for keeping the property up to code and if there is something wrong with the property that is your fault, you will be the one paying for it.

Unexpected expenses

There are a lot of situations that can result in extra money out of pocket. The water heater can suddenly break. There may be water damage in the basement. A bad tenant destroys some of the home and you have to pay for it. Maintenance fees, replacing the roof on occasion, and many other things can go wrong with the home and you will need to pay to get them taken care of for the tenant. The older the home you are dealing with the more likely you will deal with these expenses.

The best way to take care of these expenses is to set up a savings account and place some money in it each month from your rent money. This allows you to have a bit of cushion in case an unexpected expenses come up.

Bad tenants

Bad tenants are going to make your life miserable. They will often destroy at least part of the property, are difficult to get rent from, and many disappear without paying the rent for their last month. In some cases, you may need to call in a collection agency to get your money for past rent due, but often you will never see the money again. All of this can add up to costing you a lot of money and time.

Eviction expenses

Along the same line as a bad tenant, there are times you may need to evict some of your tenants. If the tenant is not paying their rent like agreed, or they have caused excessive damage to your property, it may be time to start the eviction proceedings. Filing these documents through the court and requesting the cops come to remove these individuals from the property will cost, and the landlord is required to pay the bill. In addition, the court may rule in your favor on these instances, but it is unlikely you will receive the rent due or money to fix the damages.

Having a process in place to prevent bad tenants from getting into your properties is the best way to protect your investment. Doing a background check with references, having the tenant sign a lease, and requiring a deposit that can be used if the tenant disappears or doesn't pay rent are some ways to protect your investment.

Vacancy

There are going to be times when your property will be empty. When one tenant moves on to a different town, or even to their own home, you may have a building that is empty for a bit of time. This means that you will have to foot the mortgage on your own until a new tenant moves in. Hopefully you have kept the property up nicely and it doesn't take too long for someone new to come in. Treating your tenants nicely and keeping rent at an affordable level will help you to keep the tenants around and will entice new ones to come in when needed.

Advertising fees

In order to keep your property from being vacant too long, you need to have an advertising budget. This helps prospective tenants to realize that your property is open so they can contact you to get started. If you never advertise the property, it is unlikely that anyone is ever going to move in and your property will stay vacant.

Attorney fees

There are several times when you may need to hire an attorney to help you out. They can help you to file during an eviction process when needed and will be great at drafting up tenant documents when someone new moves onto the property. You should consider how much these fees will cost and factor them into the rent if possible to ensure they don't take up your whole income.

These risks are not meant to turn you away from rental investing, but rather they should help you to understand the work that you are getting into. The good news is that most of these issues aren't going to happen to you every day. While everyone who has worked in rental properties has a story about a bad tenant, most have learned how to weed out these individuals and work to keep the best tenants in place all the time. You will learn the ropes of rental investing and can ensure that your investment is in the best shape with some more practice.

Getting the financing

Financing a rental property can be expensive. Most investors don't have the money to purchase a property outright, especially if they are going with something bigger than a single family home. For most investors, it is best to look for funding from another source to help you get started.

Rental property funding is hard to get because the banks worry that you won't be able to pay all the money back. They will take a look at your credit history, see how much you already pay in bills, including your current rent or mortgage, and they want to determine if you can afford this extra debt. While you may be planning on renting out the property to cover the new mortgage, the bank will assume you will pay it out of pocket and will check to see if your finances can handle it.

Getting your finances in line, getting rid of any bad marks on the credit score, and consider putting together a down payment can make the funding process easier. Look around to find the right funding source as well; the banks may not work the best for you, even though they have best terms in most cases, and looking at other options can make your dreams of rental property investing a reality.

Other things to consider

Before you get into rental property investing, you need to take a look at your current situation and determine how your current finances are, how much risk you are willing to take, and if this is the right investment for your personality type. Some of the other aspects of rental properties that you should consider include:

- How are your finances doing? Would you be able to support two mortgages (or a mortgage plus your current living expenses) if the property is vacant?

- If you aren't able to pay for the mortgage, are you willing to lose this property and take a major hit on your credit score, and limit your borrowing factor, in the future?

- Do you really have enough time in your schedule to be a landlord? This requires time to collect rent, check on the home, and even do repairs on the home?

- When you look at a property and figure out the expenses versus the potential income, are you really making enough money to make it worth it?

Getting into rental property investing can seem like a great way to make some money on the side, and for some people it can become a full time income, but it does require a lot of work and isn't the investment type for everyone. But for those who are willing to put in the time, can limit costs, and who would like to make a good income while building equity, rental properties can be a fantastic option!

Chapter 2:
Finding the Right Rental Property

Now that you have decided to go for rental properties as your investment choice, it is time to pick out the property that you would like to use. There are several options that you can choose including single family homes, duplexes and triplexes, apartment buildings, condos, and commercial property. Each of these provide different advantages and it is often about how much time you want to spend on the property and how much money you would like to make.

Single Family Homes

As a beginner, single family homes are the best choices to start with. They are simple to take care of and often the tenants will stick around because they can live on the property by themselves without having to get their own mortgage. If you own your home already, you have a good idea of the amount of work a single family home can take; not as much as some of the other rental properties, but it will still take up some of your time.

Benefits

- You only need to worry about one structure rather than taking care of many at one time.

- The renter will set up the utilities and you won't have to make these payments. It keeps more of the rent in your pocket.

- You can choose the home size that works best for the area. You can pick the amount of bedrooms, bathrooms, a finished basement or not, and other aspects of size.

- You will only need to keep track of one renter, one who is often reliant on handing in rent, rather than chasing after many renters.

Disadvantages

- If there are vacancies in the property, you are responsible for the mortgage since there is no one else to handle it.

- You may need multiple single family homes in order to make an income.

- You will need to take care of the outside upkeep and all the lawn work that the home needs.

Duplex and Triplex

These are also known as multi-family dwellings and can be a good middle ground between apartment buildings and single family dwellings. You will still have everyone living in one building and they are still going to attract steady tenants, but you have two, three, or four tenants helping to pay for the mortgage each month. You may find that the mortgage will still be taken care of if one unit is vacant and you will earn more of an income than with a single family option.

Benefits

- You can choose to live in part of the building and have someone else pay the rent on the other part.

- You can rent out to several tenants at a time, bringing in more income than other options.

- You still only need to take care of one building.

Disadvantages

- If you choose to stay in the building as well, you will share a wall with the renters which can make things uncomfortable at times.

- You have more units to rent out, meaning more work on your part.

- Keeping track of the utilities can take some time. You may need to have multiple utility meters or find a way to keep the payments fair for all tenants without losing money yourself.

Apartment Buildings

Apartment buildings are a big investment and most beginners will need to work up to this point. They cost more to purchase and maintain and while they can bring in a great full time income when the units are all filled, they often bring in more of the bad tenants and will have frequent vacancies that will cut into your profit. But for those who are able to maintain them well, go through background checks, and can keep the tenants in the units, apartment buildings can be a good niche.

Benefits

- Many times the investor will go with a management group for apartment buildings. This will bring in more investors and lowers the risk.

- Can make more money because more units are available. These individuals will bring the rent together to help pay off the mortgage and any costs that you incur to maintain the building.

- All the units are in one place, making it easier to maintain the outside and you can take care of all the units as needed.

Disadvantages

- There are high turnover rates in apartment buildings, meaning you will lose out on profits from these empty apartments and may need to spend more on advertising.

- For the most part, apartment buildings will require more maintenance and can take up more of your time.

- The utilities are really hard to assign without cutting into your profits. Each tenant will use a different amount of the utilities and these can change throughout each month, making it hard to predict.

Condos

There are many individuals who choose to rent out condos as their way to make money with rental property investing. The elderly are looking to move south and want a nice comfortable place to live without having to do all the upkeep and maintenance themselves. They often have a good income and are willing to pay a bit more to have a luxury place to live and someone else take care of the yardwork and the maintenance. This provides you with a great way to make a rental income as long as you are careful and do the right planning.

Benefits

- The condo is still a single unit, unless you purchase a bunch of them, so they are easy to take care o and you can either rent them out full time or provide them as a vacation rental for travelers.

- The maintenance for most condos will be taken care of through the homeowners' association, saving you time and money.

- You can have the condo be attached to your living area now, making it easier to check on tenants or you can have the tenants pay for your rent.

Disadvantages

- You will need to check with your HOA to see if renting out condos are allowed. For the most part, HOA's will allow this, especially in areas where tourists travel often, but make sure to check this early on.

- HOA is going to greatly influence what you are allowed to do on the outside of the home, such as changing the color or adding things. This can make it hard to make some of the changes you want.

- You will still be in charge of maintaining the front and backyard up to the standards set by the HOA.

- There will be neighbors here so there are some restrictions on what you are able to do to the property.

Commercial Property

If you are looking for an investment opportunity that is a bit different than the others but still offers the chance to make a good amount of money on your investment, commercial property can be the right answer. With these properties, you will be working with businesses who want to keep their physical stores in one location. This does provide some stability since many businesses don't move around often, but once a business leaves, it can be hard to find another to take its place. It also costs more to purchase a commercial property so you have to take that into consideration before starting.

Benefits
- Depending on the building you have, you can split it up and have two or more business in the same space. This provides a bigger potential of earning.

- Businesses often pay a good amount for rent. You could use this as an easier source for full time income if you choose.

Disadvantages

- If one of the tenants leaves, it is difficult to get someone else in there thanks to the popularity of online shopping.

- You must purchase liability insurance for the property, which can be really expensive.

- The investment to start out with this option is going to be much higher than the others.

- You may have to work with partners, which splits up the income, slows down decision making, and takes some of the business out of your hands.

- Maintaining a commercial property is much higher than other properties.

- It is hard to keep your tenants if you pick a property that is in the wrong area. This can be a combination of a bad area of town or one that is just too far away to be convenient for the customers.

Chapter 3:
Getting the Home Ready to Lease

Now that you have chosen the property you would like to use for your rental investment, it is time to get the home prepared for renting out. To start, go into the home with the eyes of a prospective renter. What would you like to see done in the home to make it more comfortable? Are there things that would make you want to stay in the property? Are there things that you turn you off? The things that create a negative response in the renter are some of the first ones that you should take care of to ensure the potential renter is willing to live in your property.

Some of the items that you should take extra precautions of fixing and taking care of to make a rental property look amazing include:

Fix what is broken

If you got a really good deal on the property, there are probably a few things that you need to fix up around the home. Maybe a little bit of paint is needed, fixing a few spots on the walls, or adding some new appliances that actually work. When purchasing the home, there are things you should have taken into consideration while picking the price, but make sure that they get done before a potential renter comes to look at the property.

Get the home up to code

There are certain codes that every home needs to have before you are allowed to rent to others. If you fail to fix any code violations in the home, or you don't get new violations fixed as soon as possible, your tenant could sue you and your investment will go into the ground. Hopefully you had an inspection done on the property before purchasing which would catch most of these violations and save you the headache.

Even after the property is rented out, it is a good idea to schedule regular checks of some important features in the home, such as electricity, water, and the heater. Set up a time during the year with your tenant where you can have the professionals come in and take a look at these systems to prevent anything happening. This is a great way to provide service to the tenant while protecting your investment.

Change the locks

You should change all the codes for the home and garage as well as change the locks on all doors to the outside, including gates, sheds, and mailboxes. This ensures that only you and the tenant have the keys to the property and that no one else is able to get in. You should do this process each time a tenant moves out so that no one who is unauthorized to be around can get into the property.

Clean the carpets

It is wroth your time to call a professional in to take care of the carpets. Full steam and a shampoo of the property can help to brighten up the carpets, gets rid of old stains and all the dirt, and can make the whole house look and feel better. You can choose to do this on your own, but the professionals are often able to do a better clean and can be amazing if your home has a musty or other off odor inside.

Work on the yard

The yard is one of the first things that a potential renter is going to see about the property. It is worth your time to make the yard look as nice as possible. Make sure the lawn is mowed, trim any bushes and trees on the property, pull out the weeds, fix anything that is broken, remove anything that is dying, and even consider adding some new flowers or other greenery to the yard to make it look better. Spraying off the sidewalk to remove dirt and keeping leaves and other items out of the yard can make it look so much better.

Change out the filters

The filters can get dirty really dirty over time and they can affect how well the ventilation system works in the home. make sure to replace the filters on a regular basis, clean out the vents, and even the ceiling areas. It is also a good idea to get rid of any reusable filters and use disposable ones instead. The disposable ones aren't going to require you to clean them all the time, making it easier to maintain.

Clean the interior

You would be surprised at how much a good cleaning can do to make the home look better. It is often best to go with a professional service because they will catch more dirt and grime than you can on your own. Make sure that the walls are wiped down, the windows cleaned, all the appliances are cleaned out, and the floors are taken care of. It may take some time, but a potential tenant will notice if there is a lot of dirt and grime in the home and it could turn them away.

Find ways to let the lights in

A dark home can be a big turn off for some renters. They don't want to live in a place that is too dark and since this will make the property look smaller than it is, you could be using out on some rental income for something so simple. If there are any lightbulbs that have gone out in the home or are broken, make sure to replace them right away. Clean off the windows and find a way to draw back the sashes to let in more light in most of the rooms. Consider finding brighter bulbs and going with some lighter paint colors to make the home look a little lighter.

Check the ceiling fans

This is an area a lot of home owners forget to clean. But the top of the ceiling fans can get really dusty in no time. First, get a wipe and learn how to clean off the tops of each fan, both on the inside and outside of the home, and then take some time to see if they are all working properly or if you need to replace the blades or something else to make it work better.

Check those screens

Next it is on to the windows and doors. If your current windows and main doors don't have screens in place, it is a good idea to invest in some. You can measure out the spaces that you need and go to your local hardware store to find the replacements that will work the best for you. This is a great selling point because homeowners will want to open up their windows and not have all the bugs and dust get inside.

If there are screens in the windows and doors, you should inspect all of them. See if there are any rips, tears, or holes in the screen and replace any that you are not able to easily repair. Also check and make sure that they fit into the windows properly and air is not able to get through on the sides. Wipe down the edges to make them look nice and clean.

Spray for the pests

Depending on the age of the home, you may find that there are a lot of pests inside. Homes that are in certain areas or homes that haven't had someone live inside them for some time often have pests who get in and try to make the property their home. Spraying for pests can help to make the home more comfortable and will scare away all those pests. Even if the home has had someone living inside it when you purchased, it is still a good idea to go through and spray for pests to be sure the property is ready.

Paint, fix, and repair

First, go through and find any of the holes that are in the walls. Most of these will simply come from the previous owner putting nails in the wall to hang things, but any bigger holes should be taken care of as well. After this is done, you should paint the walls a fresh coat to make them look and feel better. Neutral colors are often the best because they will appeal to the most amount of people possible.

These little fixes will often take just a few minutes each to get done, but they will make a big difference in how the potential tenant views the property. And whether you will be able to get market value out of the property. The best part is a lot of these fixes won't require a ton of money on your part, maybe some paint and cleaning supplies, and yet it will add a lot of value to your home. Take the time to look for simple fixes that will make a big difference in the appearance of the property to help entice those tenants to come in.

Chapter 4:
How Much Should I Charge in Rent?

Once the property is all fixed up and ready to take in a new tenant, it is time to figure out how much you would like to charge for rent. Of course, you want to make as much profit as possible after paying for your mortgage and other expenses, but if the property is not at market value, you are going to have a hard time bringing the tenants in.

The first thing that you will need to look at is how much you are going to spend in expenses to maintain the home. This would include the amount that you are paying for the mortgage each month, the taxes, and the insurance for the home. You may also want to put a bit of the rent bac each month to use whenever something breaks or needs repair in the property. This number should be lower than what you will charge for rent so that you can make a profit.

Once you have this number, you need to determine how much you would like to earn in profit each month. You should be reasonable with this number. If you have a single family home, you will not make a thousand dollars each month from renting this out. Keep it modest and in line with how many tenants you plan to have inside the property.

Market value of the home will make a big difference in how much you choose to charge for rent. If the market value keeps your rent for homes that are similar to yours at $900 a month, you should stay somewhere around this number. Tenants are not going to want to pay higher because they can find another place to stay that falls in line better and they may see it as a waste of money.

Hopefully, you did the calculations about your property before making the purchase to determine if the market rate for rent on similar properties would be enough to cover your costs of owning the home. For example, if you have to pay $950 a month for mortgage, insurance, and taxes and you are only able to charge $900 a month to get tenants inside, you are going to lose money on the endeavor.

On the other hand, if you are able to keep your mortgage, insurance, and taxes down to $700 a month, you could still place the rent at $900 and make a profit in the process. It all just depends on where the market value of your home is and how much you owe in expenses.

Ideally, you purchased the home at a below market value. This makes it easier to get the rent to line up right. If the home price is too close to the market value, it is going to be a challenge to price the rent high enough to make a profit. The lower you can get the purchase price to be in these instances, the easier it is to make a good profit. Make sure you go through all these calculations before purchasing so you aren't stuck with a rental property that won't earn you an income.

If you are unsure about the market price for similar rentals, make sure to check online or your local government office. Charts about average rental income in the area will be listed here for you to look over and it can make it so much easier to determine where a comfortable rental price will be. Try to stay as close to these numbers as possible to entice the good tenants while still making as much profit as possible.

Chapter 5:
Finding Good Tenants and Creating a Lease

Finding good tenants

Finding good tenants can make all the difference when starting out in rental properties. Good tenants are the ones who pay their rent on time, take care of the property, and only call when there is something legitimately wrong with the property that you need to fix. They stick around for a long time and when it is time to move on, they have kept the place so nice that you are able to send back the deposit to them.

Finding these good tenants is a bit of a challenge though. Even people who have done rental property investing have stories about horrible tenants, so being on the lookout to avoid these bad tenants should be top priority for you as a beginner. While you may not be able to avoid a bad tenant every time, taking the right precautions will make it less likely that the bad tenants will get into your property.

The first thing you need to do is list the home. Do a good job with taking pictures to really showcase how great the property is. Most good tenants are drawn to properties that look nice, have been well maintained, and are in nice neighborhoods. Having some good pictures of the property can help to entice these good tenants right away. Post on a few different rental sites to increase the odds of being seen.

When listing the property, make sure to write out some of the requirements of living in the property. For example, list the rental price, how long the lease will last, and the security deposit. This avoids confusion later on and can save you time for answering the same questions from potential renters all the time.

Once you start getting some applications in for the property, it is time to look at each one individually. They may all look great on paper, but since most applications don't go too in depth about personal information, it is easy for some bad tenants to make themselves look good on this step. As the landlord, you need to take precautions and double check the information first.

A good way to check on the applicants is to do a background check. This allows you to see a bit of their credit history, such as if they've paid their rent on time in the past and some of their work history. You can also see past landlords, whether they may not be able to pay the rent well, and other factors that can help you make a good determination.

The good news is that telling potential renters that you will perform a background check on them right from the beginning can really help to keep away some of the bad tenants. These tenants realize what is on their background check and will assume you won't rent to them, so will pick another property. This isn't true about all tenants, but it can help to keep a few of them away. And for those bad tenants who decide to try it anyway, you will be able to catch the holes in their application and see that they don't pay their bills on time pretty quickly.

You can choose to do the background checks yourself, but it is usually easier and faster to hire a company who can do it for you. Find one who can get the job done quickly, without costing too much so you can see the results and get a new tenant in the property.

Another thing to consider is asking your tenants for references. Make sure that they are not family members of the tenant. Something like a past landlord, coworker, or professional acquaintance is a much better option. Bad tenants usually have a hard time finding three or four references who would speak highly of them and they will either avoid providing these to you, or you will talk to the references and realize that this tenant is not right for you.

Many beginners are eager to fill up their property and will take the first tenant who fills out an application. This plan is risky; sometimes it will result in a great tenant who will pay their rent on time and take care of the property, but most likely you will end up with a bad tenant who makes you never want to do rental properties again. Doing background checks and asking for references can make the difference between finding a bad tenant or finding a good one who can make this investment worth your time.

Creating a lease

Creating a lease is one of the best things you can do to protect your investment. It helps protect both you and the tenant, helping both to understand the responsibilities of each party. Never let someone into the property without first going over and having them sign the lease. You can create your own lease or hire an attorney to help you create a legal document. Some of the things that you should include in the lease are:

- The terms of the agreement—if you discussed something with the tenant, make sure that it is written into the lease. Writing helps to make the words legal and can ensure that everyone is on the same page.

- Identify the parties—clearly state who the landlord and tenant are as well as the physical address of the property in question.

- Duration of the lease—this document should contain information on how long the lease will last. Most residential leases will last a year, but some landlords chose to go with six months, three months, or even two years. Provide which date the lease begins on and when it will end to help avoid confusion. Include information on renewing the lease after that period ends.

- Rental price—the lease should list how much the rent is each month. If you expect the rent to be paid in a particular form (cash, check or other option), say this in the lease.

- Security deposit—write out the security deposit that the tenant must pay. Many landlords will leave this part blank and fill it in later so they can offer promotions (such as a lowered security deposit), to bring more tenants in.

- List what each person will pay for—if you are including the utilities, or even part of the utilities, in the price of rent, list that out. If you require that the tenant takes care of everything, list it out in the lease.

- Have a section about subleasing—most landlords will not allow subleasing of their property. This is when the tenant finds someone else to lease out the property, usually charging the new tenant more to make a profit. Include a clause in the lease stating this is not allowed and that new individuals are not allowed to move in without first notifying the landlord.

- Dispute resolution—provide information to the tenant on how to resolve disputes that may come up. You can provide them with information on who to contact, point them to the right forms to fill out, or other information to ensure the dispute is taken care of.

- Lease termination—there may be times when the landlord or the tenant wishes to terminate the lease. List these exceptions in the lease right from the beginning. Also, list any financial consequences of the tenant if they break their lease improperly.

You can choose to write up the lease yourself using a template found online. This is usually a less expensive way to go about writing up the lease, but sometimes the legality of it can be questioned. Talking to an attorney can be a better option. They can help you draft up a legal lease that you can use for all of your tenants and answer any questions that you have concerning what to put into the lease.

Remember that while a lease may not seem necessary at the time, it is a good way to protect you and the tenant. You have some security knowing how long the tenant will be in the property, or at least be compensated if they leave early, and options if they destroy the property as well. The tenant has the peace of mind knowing that you won't kick them out for undue reasons, their rent will stay the same, and that you will take good care of the property while they are living inside. While the lease may seem like a pain to go through and sign, it is really protection for both parties.

Chapter 6:
You as the Landlord

As the landlord, you will be responsible for some things as well. This process requires more than just purchasing the property and waiting for the check to come in at the end of the month. The tenant will expect that you do some work to help maintain the property and you must follow any landlord-tenant laws in your area.

Your responsibilities as a landlord

You expect the tenant to keep the property in good shape and pay their rent, but the tenant also expects you to keep up your end of the bargain as well. You can't sit back and wait for the rental check each month without helping the tenant out, keeping the property in good shape, and following other landlord laws in your state. While the rules are different in each state, there are five parts that most of these laws are broken down to.

Manage the security deposit

The landlord does have the right to charge a security deposit, but it is not the property of the landlord. Instead, it is a security blanket for the landlord that they have to hold in a trust. If the tenant pays the rent and keeps the property in good working order, the landlord must return the security deposit when the tenant moves out. But if the tenant doesn't pay the rent or causes some damage to the property, the landlord can use the money to help recover some of the costs. Follow your local laws in terms of maximum security deposit allowed, how to store the deposit, how to return the deposit, and what happens to the deposit if you happen to sell the property.

Obligation to disclose the owner

All tenants have a right to know some information about who owns the property. The landlord should release the names and the addresses of those who manage the building, make repairs, collect rent, and who will handle any complaints. This disclosure is given in writing and the landlord will provide the information before the tenant moves in. If there are changes in any of these, the landlord must notify the tenant.

Obligation of possession of the unit

This one basically means that the landlord will have the unit vacant and ready for the tenant on the agreed upon move in date. While you can show the property while someone else is still living inside it, the unit must be completely vacant when the new tenant moves in. If you don't have the unit ready, the tenant could pursue legal action.

In addition to this, the landlord is able to pursue legal action if a squatter or someone else who isn't allowed to live in the unit, is found inside the unit. If the landlord wins, they could be given damages for this time and effort.

Maintain the Property

The landlord is the one who is responsible for maintaining the property. While the tenant is not allowed to purposely destroy the property and must only have normal wear and tear on the property, the landlord is in charge for keeping the property habitable, safe, and clean. They must frequently check that the property is up to code, come in and perform the repairs that are required, provide trash receptacles, and running water in the properties, and perform other actions as agreed upon in the lease.

Limitation of liability

The landlord must follow through on any agreements made in the lease as well as those that are listed in the landlord-tenant law. This liability is done once the landlord sells the property as long as they notify the tenant that the property is now under new management or ownership. The new landlord will take over the liability to adhere to the terms in the lease agreement. If the new landlord wishes to make changes to the lease agreement, they must provide this information in writing to the tenant and provide the tenant time to make adjustments if they wish to not follow these new terms.

Each state and local area will have variations on these laws and it is important to check with these to ensure you are holding up your end of the landlord-tenant bargain and to prevent costly expenses on your part. Keeping your tenant happy and following the laws set in place will help you to save money in the long run.

Growing your portfolio

After some time has passed, you will find that you can make a steady income with rental properties and may have even set some money aside to help with a down payment on another building. Once you are comfortable with your current workload and ready to take on more, it may be time to grow the portfolio and add on more rental properties to earn more money.

You should follow the same steps for your second or third property as you did with your first. Find a good property that fits into your budget and won't require too much work. Remember that you already have one rental property to look after and add that into how much you will be able to handle with more properties. Also consider if you would be able to cover all the costs if both properties are vacant at the same time.

Over time, you will grow your portfolio quite a bit and may have many rental properties under your name. You can choose to have this become your full time income and devote yourself to taking care of these properties and keeping the tenants happy. Sometimes, the portfolio will grow big enough that you will chose to go with a management company to get all the work done. The possibilities are endless and if you work hard and manage your properties well, you can easily start to make a great income from your rental properties.

Chapter 7:
Tips for a Beginner in Rental Properties

As a beginner in this area, you want to make sure that you are taking the proper steps to really grow your rental business. There are a lot of mistakes that you can inadvertently make if you're not careful, but over time, you will learn the process that is right for you and you can really start to make a great income. Some of the tips that you as a beginner should follow when starting out on rental properties include:

- Realize that you aren't an expert right now—no one starts out in real estate as an expert in the field. Most barely know what they are doing, but with some research, doing your homework, and getting out into the field, it becomes easier than ever to learn on the job.

- Do your research—research can make a break your business. Too many people assume that starting in real estate is easy, but with a bit of research, they may find that their chosen property is in the wrong area, they can't get enough rent to cover the mortgage, and so much more. Always do your homework and find out as much information about the area, the market, and more before jumping in.

- Speak with other investors—these investors will offer invaluable tools to how to get started. They will answer your questions and can often point you in the right direction when it comes to properties to try out, tricks to fix up the property, and more!

- Have some creativity—too many times a new investor will look at a property and only see numbers. This is important to making sure that the investment is worth your time, but it can also leave some good properties behind. If you can think outside the box in terms of financing, fixing up the property, and more, you open the door to more options.

- Learn how to sacrifice—you won't be able to get into rental investing and go on two or three vacations a year. You should put that money into a down payment or into fixing up the home. You may need to make some sacrifices during the first few years while you get the investment started. The good news though is that once the investments start to bring money back to you, you can easily go on that big trip!

- Write out your plan—there is something about writing out your plans and having them down on paper that makes a big difference. Write down as much information about your plan as possible. Include business income, expected revenue, expenses, and even how much you plan to lose on this each year. This helps to keep you focused and on track for the best success.

- Good bookkeeping makes the difference—don't wait until the end of the year to get your bookkeeping in line. This is going to be a mess and can easily cause issues during tax time. Instead, focus on getting started with the bookkeeping before you even pick your first property. Working on it in your personal life can help translate it over to your new business. If you just can't do the bookkeeping well, hire a professional for you. It makes all the difference in the world when doing taxes and getting the best deductions.

- Give yourself some time—you are not going to make a full time income with rental properties right from the beginning. Most investors start out with one property and keep working their day jobs for the first few years. Over time you can add in more properties and eventually is may be possible to replace your full time income. But this is not going to happen overnight. It is recommended that you take five years to reach success. Some people will reach success in a year or two, but give yourself some time before giving up.

- Get background checks done—anyone who has worked in rental properties knows that a bad tenant can be a nightmare. They don't pay rent, they mess up the property, and you could lose thousands in a short time. While background checks aren't always accurate indicators, they make it easier to catch tenants who will cause trouble.

- Realize the property will be empty sometimes—it is a nice dream to assume your property will always have a tenant, but this isn't the case. Even long term tenants will move out at some point so having a plan in place to cover the mortgage and other costs of the home when no one is paying rent can help out. Putting a bit back in savings each month can help you out if there are times of vacancy in the property.

- Get a lease—never trust someone by their word. You are running a business and should have a legal lease in place with every tenant. This helps to protect you if the tenant does something wrong in the property, like destroying it or not paying their rent. It also protects the tenant because the lease will outline what you as the landlord are expected to do as well. Always have a lease signed and on file for every tenant.

- Take care of the tenant—your job is not done the second the tenant signs a lease. You need to take care of them and the property as well. If something is wrong with the property, get over there and fix it as soon as possible. If you need to come to the property, give the tenant a bit of notice (even if it is to do some maintenance such as changing air filters). If you treat the tenant with respect, they are more likely to stay around for longer.

- Keep up to date on state and housing codes. It is easy to purchase a property, but there are codes that you have to take into consideration if you want a tenant to live there. If you don't meet these codes, your tenant can sue you. Make sure to check these local codes in your area since they are different in each town.

Working in rental properties is not easy. This is why it is recommended to just start out with one or two small properties until you understand the workflow and know how much you are able to handle. As the landlord, you are responsible for picking out good tenants as well as maintaining the property and keeping it up to code.

This is a full time job with just a few properties to manage. But when you do your research and slowly build up the empire, you will be able to make a great income with rental properties without feeling too overwhelmed.

Conclusion

Thank for making it through to the end of *book*, let's hope it was informative and able to provide you with all of the tools you need to achieve your goals whatever it may be.

The next step is to get started on your rental property investment. You will need to go out and find the right property that meets your needs and will provide you with a great side, or full, income. Once you have made the match, it is time to get to work fixing up the property and getting it up to code to help make it safe and comfortable for any prospective tenant. Probably one of the hardest parts of this investment is finding a good tenant and getting the lease set up properly, but with a good background check and other tips found in this guidebook, it is easier than ever to bring in that great tenant.

Getting started in rental properties is not easy. You have to put in a lot of work to maintain the properties and find tenants who will pay rent for your income. But the work can be some of the most rewarding work you will do in your life and once you get a little experience, it won't take long before you add more to your portfolio and replace your full time income. This guidebook provides you with the suggestions and tools you need to make this a reality.

Finally, if you found this book useful in anyway, a review on Amazon is always appreciated!